Waymarkers

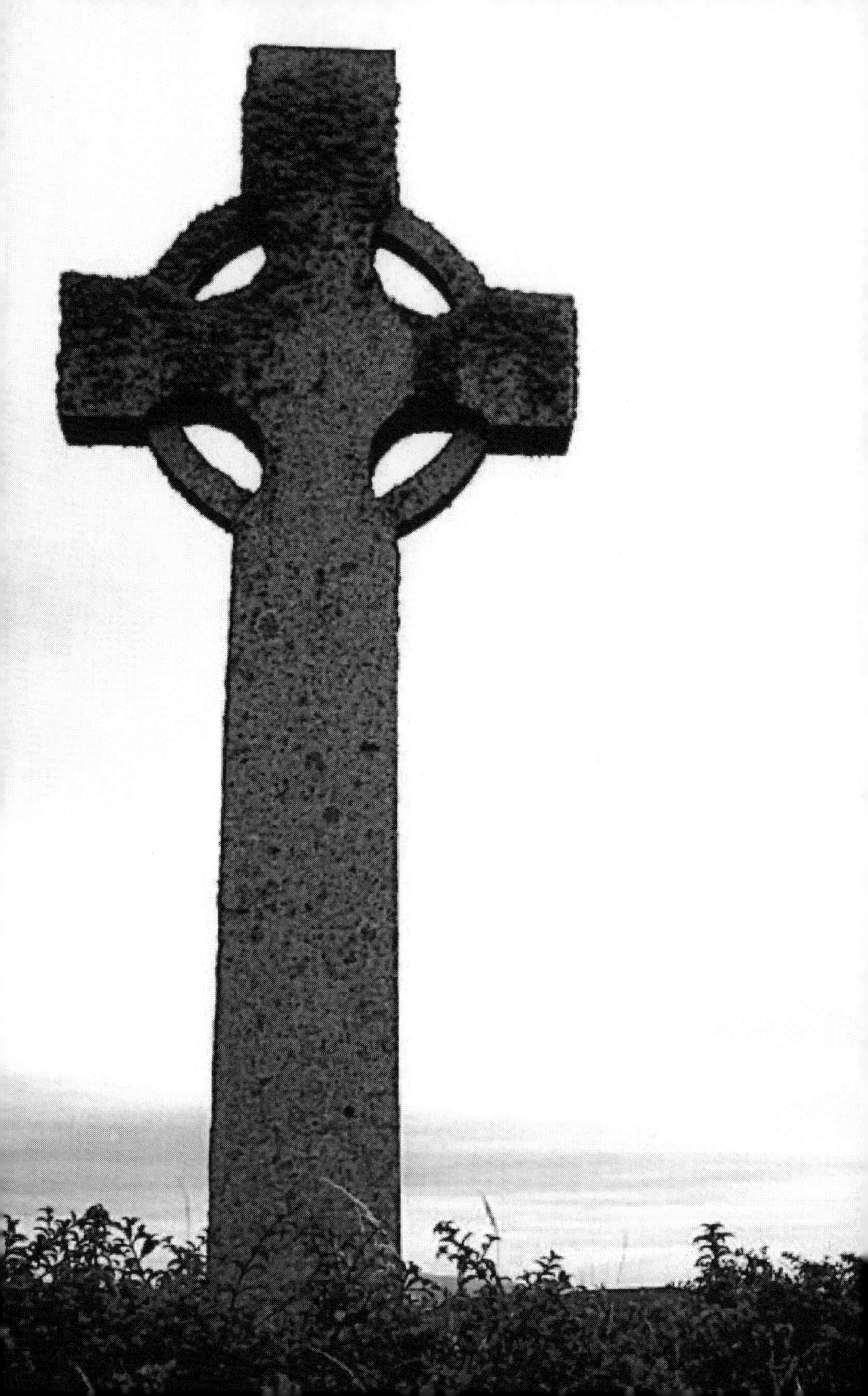

Waymarkers

Collected Prayers, Poems & Reflections
for the Preparation and Pilgrimage to Iona

Written and compiled by Mary A. DeJong

"We will come back changed. Of that I am certain. But of course that is why you go on pilgrimage in the first place, to find the holy, stumble upon God in action, and be changed forever by the experience."
-*Cannon Trevor Dennis*

ACKNOWLEDGMENTS

The author is grateful to reprint with permission of their authors or publishers the following:

'A Place of Hope' by Peter Miller is taken from *An Iona Prayer Book* published by Canterbury Press © Canterbury Press, 1998. Used by permission of Hymns Ancient & Modern Ltd. Peter Millar, *An Iona Prayer Book* (Canterbury Press, Norwich, 1998), p.6.; Vivienne Hull-quote; Robert Fulghum, *Third Wish* (Becker & Mayer, Bellevue, WA, 2009); *Pilgrimage to Nidaros. A Practical Pilgrimage Theology* (Liturgical Centre, Trondheim, 2003), 185; J. Philip Newell, *Celtic Prayers from Iona,* (Paulist Press, New York, 1997), various; Blessings (various), Reprinted from *In the Sanctuary of Women* by Jan Richardson. © 2010 by Upper Room Books. Used by permission from Upper Room Books. To order, phone 1.800.972.0433 or go to www.upperroom.org/bookstore; Lyanda Lynn Haupt-quote, *Crow Planet,* (Little, Brown, and Company, 2009). Used by permission.

Every effort has been made to acknowledge authors of their work, and acknowledge copyright holders of all the quotations included. Apologies for any errors or omissions that may remain, and would ask those concerned to contact the editor, who will ensure that full acknowledgment is made in the future.

The Scripture quotations contained herein are from the New Revised Standard Version Bible, copyright © 1989, Division of Christian Education of the National Council of the Churches of Christ in the United States of America. Used by permission. All rights reserved.

Copy editing by Kristina Kennedy Davis, kDavis@godinternational.org
Jacket and book design by Joel DeJong

Copyright © Mary A. DeJong., 2011, All rights reserved.
www.waymarkers.net
THIRD EDITION
ISBN 978 4563 5112 0
Printed in the United States of America

*For all your journeys
and for Joel, who inspires and gives
me courage to continue my own*

Bless to us, O God,
The earth beneath our feet,
Bless to us, O God,
The path whereon we go,
Bless to us, O God,
The people whom we meet.

*-Based on an old prayer from the
Outer Hebrides*

CONTENTS

Author's Note • 15
Introduction: Iona • 17
Pilgrimage-Sacred Travel • 29
Pilgrimage: The Longing • 32
Pilgrimage: The Calling • 34
Pilgrimage: The Departure-Separation • 36
Pilgrimage: The Pilgrim's Way-Crossing the Threshold • 40
Pilgrimage: The Labyrinth-Transformation • 42
Pilgrimage: Arrival • 46
Pilgrimage: Reincorporation-Bringing Back the Boon • 49
Waymarker: Flying • 53
Waymarker: Glasgow-Bus • 59
Waymarker: The Rail • 63
Waymarker: Mull-Ferry • 66
Waymarker: Mull-Bus • 71
Waymarker: Iona-Ferry • 77
Waymarker: Home Again • 83
Pilgrimage Centering Tools • 87

AUTHOR'S NOTE

To make pilgrimage is to intentionally prepare for a passage that will inevitably change one's life. *Waymarkers* is divided into three sections to support this transformation. The first section provides helpful generalized information and guiding materials related to the stages of pilgrimage. I hope that this section will be of assistance while you plan and prepare for your journey to Iona.
The second section is written to highlight the waymarkers one encounters while actually en route to this particular sacred site. You will find guided reflections specific to the multiple and various legs specific to this trip. Lastly, I have compiled helpful centering tools that I have used both personally and in my retreat work on Iona. My gratitude is deep and wide for those whose extensive work has impacted my life, this project, and the journeys of so many others.

Waymarkers was inspired by my own personal pilgrimage to Iona in 2009. I carried an intention, a question, whose answer became clear in September 2010 with the birth of my third child, Annette Persis. It is with an absolute humble heart that I offer to you my intentions for *Waymarkers*: prepare and make well the journey. Your life will be forever changed by this pilgrimage.

Godspeed.

-Mary A. DeJong
Seattle, WA

Stand by the roads and look, and ask for the ancient paths, where the good way is; and walk in it,
and find rest for your souls. Jeremiah 6:16 (ESV)

INTRODUCTION: IONA

Iona. *Iona*. The name itself has a special quality-the way it personalizes you as you begin to say the isle's name, and then flows roundly through your mouth ending at the tip of your tongue. *Iona*. The –n– sound is warm, comforting; just by saying the name of this small island, one wants to go there. *Iona*. And for hundreds and hundreds of years pilgrims have gone to this place looking for warmth and comfort from the One who named *you*.

For a host of reasons, both historically and geographically, Iona, Scotland is a particular place, a small sanctuary-like island seemingly hanging onto the skirt of the known world. Many of the compelling motives to visit this isle are attached to various prophecies attributed to Columba-founder of the great center of monasticism and evangelism on Iona. One such prophetic foretelling was made on the evening before the monastery's founding father died, in the year 597. Small and humble though this island was, he said, it would in time be regarded by the kings and commoners of many lands as a place of great and special honor. The saint's prediction has indeed proved true. E. Mairi MacArthur has accomplished an extensive study on this island and its history; she concisely tells the story of this island's significance with these words:

This speck of rock and turf in the Hebridean sea, little more than three and a half miles long by one mile wide, rapidly assumed deep spiritual significance for the peoples of Scotland and Ireland, their stories bound together through the personage of Columcille or St. Columba. Some of their early

Glorious it is when wandering time is come.
--Eskimo song

INTRODUCTION: IONA

kings were brought for burial in Iona's hallowed soil as, later, were many of the great chiefs of [Gaelic speaking-Scotland]. Over the centuries the island became the destination of pilgrims from, ultimately, every Christian denomination. Its ecclesiastical remains, carved stones and high crosses have been visited and interpreted by countless antiquarians, archaeologists, theologians, historians, writers and artists. Down the years, textbooks and travel guides have tended to echo the sentiments of Samuel Johnson, that Iona was above all 'that illustrious island', inspiring piety in all.[1]

The journey itself to Iona makes this place unique; it is long, quite complicated and even relatively uncomfortable for the urbanite who is accustomed to quick and easy travel. This distance provides the perfect pilgrimage process, for it truly requires a removal of oneself from all that is familiar and supplies a lengthy trek–full of obstacles, no doubt! Once there, one finds a sparsely populated island, with almost no cars and a large abbey, whose structure appears to have dropped from the heavens onto this topographically small and relatively insignificant place. Sheep outnumber the residents and the sunlight plays on the hillsides in the most magical ways. One senses almost immediately Iona is indeed a "thin space" – that brushing up against the Divine is inevitable.

Iona also has a remarkable history; the community Columba founded there was the direct ancestor of much of the Christian Church in Scotland. Historians and scholars also widely agree that Iona was the likely place of origin of the

INTRODUCTION: IONA

famous Book of Kells, a manuscript Gospel book, known for its striking illuminated letters and knot work, which are great examples of Celtic Christian design. The island has a remarkably continuous religious history and significance, which stretches from pre-Christian times through the Celtic monastic settlement and its Benedictine and Augustinian successors down to the present day Iona Community and the restoration of the medieval abbey buildings in the twentieth century. There is an equally long tradition of pilgrimage to 'the place of Columba'. This is evidenced by the stacked stones, called cairns, on the beach of St. Columba's Bay that appear to have been constructed by medieval pilgrims as acts of devotion.[2]

Iona has a unique and challenging call to modern pilgrims. Whereas in the past, pilgrims would seek to rise above their physical nature to engage and experience God, today we must seek to integrate all of creation to live a more pure and holy existence. By going to Iona we are looking to learn from a place and a faith tradition that honors this interconnectivity; our prayer is that we might leave bringing this harmony back home with us so that we might live inspired on behalf of Others and the future of our world.

This collection of guiding materials, prayers, poems, and meditations aims to provide the pilgrim journeying to Iona with means to guide reflections both in preparation and en route to this sacred site.

INTRODUCTION: IONA

"To become a pilgrim is to be understood as a way of looking at life itself: constantly moving and willing to break away from fixed ideas about oneself and others, breaking away from lifestyles that do not respect the earth as a community of all living creatures. The pilgrim realizes that there is a change to undergo, and afterwards the return home with extended faith and understanding of life. The outer physical landscape people wander through with all its varying scenery is, in the pilgrim's tradition, understood as a picture of the inner landscape every person carries with them."

-Arne Bakken

INTRODUCTION: IONA

To the Pilgrim

Set out!
You were born for the road
Set out!
You have a meeting to keep.
Where? With whom?
Perhaps with yourself.

Set out!
Your steps will be your words-
The road your song,
The weariness your prayers.
And at the end
Your silence will speak to you.

Set out!
Alone, or with others-
But get out of yourself!
You have created rivals-
You will find companions.
You envisaged enemies-
You will find brothers and sisters.

INTRODUCTION: IONA

Set out!
Your head does not know
Where your feet are leading your heart.

Set out!
You were born for the road-
The pilgrim's road.
Someone is coming to meet you-
Is seeking you
In the shrine at the end of the road-
In the shrine at the depths of your heart.

God is your peace.
God is your joy!

Go!
God already walks with you!
-Anonymous

INTRODUCTION: IONA

Ithaka

As you set out for Ithaka
hope your road is a long one,
full of adventure, full of discover.
Laistrygonians, Cyclops,
angry Poseidon-don't be afraid of them:
you'll never find things like that on your way
as long as you keep your thoughts raised high,
as long as a rare excitement
stirs your spirit and your body.
Laistrygonians, Cyclops,
wild Poseidon-you won't encounter them
unless you bring them along inside your soul,
unless your soul sets them up in front of you.

Hope your road is a long one.
May there be many summer mornings when,
with what pleasure, what joy,
you enter harbors you're seeing for the first time;
may you stop at Phoenician trading stations
to buy fine things,
mother of pearl and coral, amber and ebony,
sensual perfume of every kind-
as many sensual perfumes as you can;

INTRODUCTION: IONA

and may you visit many Egyptian cities
to learn and go on learning from their scholars.

Keep Ithaka always in your mind.
Arriving there is what you're destined for.
But don't hurry the journey at all.
Better if it lasts for years,
so you're old by the time you reach the island,
wealthy with all you've gained on the way,
not expecting Ithaka to make you rich.
Ithaka gave you the marvelous journey.
Without her you wouldn't have set you.
She has nothing left to give you now.

And if you find her poor, Ithaka won't have fooled you.
Wise as you will have become, so full of experience,
you'll have understood by then what these Ithakas mean.
-C.P. Cavafy (1863-1933)

INTRODUCTION: IONA

Blessing for the Traveler

Every time you leave home,
Another road take you
Into a world you were never in.

New strangers on other paths await.
New places that have never seen you
Will startle a little at your entry.
Old places that know you well
Will pretend nothing
Changed since your last visit.

When you travel, you find yourself
Alone in a different way,
More attentive now
To the self you bring along,
Your more subtle eye watching
You abroad; and how what meets you
Touches that part of the heart
That lies low at home:

How you unexpectedly attune
To the timbre in some voice,
Opening a conversation
You want to take in
To where your longing
Has pressed hard enough
Inward, on some unsaid dark,

INTRODUCTION: IONA

To create a crystal of insight
You could not have known
You needed
To illuminate
Your way.

When you travel,
A new silence
Goes with you,
And if you listen,
You will hear
What your heart would
Love to say.

A journey can become a sacred thing:
Make sure, before you go,
To take the time
To bless your going forth,
To free your heart of ballast
So that the compass of your soul
Might direct you toward
The territories of spirit
Where you will discover
More of your hidden life,
And the urgencies
That deserve to claim you.

May you travel in an awakened way,
Gathered wisely into your inner ground;

INTRODUCTION: IONA

That you may not waste the invitations
Which wait along the way to transform you.

May you travel safely, arrive refreshed,
And live your time away to its fullest;
Return home more enriched, and free
To balance the gift of days which call you.
-*John O'Donohue, To Bless the Space Between Us*

Since we are travelers and pilgrims in the world, let us ever ponder on the end of the road, that is our life, for the end of our roadway is our home.
-Columban, sermon

PILGRIMAGE: SACRED TRAVEL

You are setting out to make pilgrimage-one of the most ancient forms of journey for people of faith from all cultures and religions. While this word may sound antiquated and seemingly irrelevant to modern-day Christians, there is an awakening sense that making a pilgrimage is a way to find answers to your deepest questions and experience a spirit-renewing ritual. This type of journey invites the traveler to see the sacred in every step and in every turn. With a deepening of focus, keen preparation, attention to the path below your feet, and respect for the destination at hand, it is possible to transform even the most ordinary trip into a sacred journey, a pilgrimage.[3]

Spiritual journeys take us to the sacred sites of our past, of our world, and of our imagination. The earliest recorded pilgrimage is attributed to Abraham, who wandered from ancient Ur through the desert seeking God almost 4,000 years ago. Descendants of Abraham continued this tradition of setting out from home on a sacred journey to find God and an inspired way of living. Sacred texts from all religions, the Bible, the Torah, and the Quran, admonish their followers to gather at the birthplaces and tombs of the prophets, the sites where miracles occurred, or the paths they walked in search of enlightenment.[4] As early as the fourth and fifth centuries there is evidence of people leaving their homeland to walk along the "glory road" to the Holy Land so they might travel in the footsteps of Christ. Traveling to Israel today is still one of the most popular, sacred trips for people of faith; there is an inherent longing to return to these landscapes where the

What matters on our journey is –
how deeply you see, how attentively you hear, how richly the encounters are felt in your heart and soul.
-Phil Cousineau

PILGRIMAGE: SACRED TRAVEL

*Before you,
beside you,
behind you,
may Christ our
Light attend
your way.*

Holy One walked and miracles happened. Being *there* and touching the soil with our own hands spurs the imagination and buttresses the spirit to live in a divinely transformed way.

As you travel, engage your pilgrimage from the perspective of the sacred journey's "universal round"; engage and explore the spiritual dimensions of the archetypal stages that take us from home, to journey, to arrival, to back home again. Like the centuries-old knot work of the ancient Celts, the journey is likened to the thread that wanders far from the center, and then spins back in again. What results from this design is not only beautiful art, but a profound way to see life's journey as a single, unbroken thread weaving in and over itself, returning and going out from the center, creating an overall image of guided, inspired living.

The pilgrim's motives have always been manifold: to pay homage, to fulfill a vow or obligation, to do penance, to be rejuvenated spiritually, or to feel the release of catharsis. The motive-or intention-behind the journey must be declared, and to name it is essential. With it, the pilgrim commits both the trip and her posture to that of prayer and intentional listening. Everything surrounding the journey is sacred, even the seemingly mundane elements of travel. The heart and soul of the pilgrimage is to bring about an encounter with God that will result in a changed and different life.

The experience of the journey begins with a deep disturbance-*The Longing*, which is the first stage of the pilgrimage. From

PILGRIMAGE: SACRED TRAVEL

this moment we must be listening for the knock, for *The Call* that will name our pilgrimage and give shape to our sacred intention. *Departure*, or *Separation*, is the third stage of pilgrimage where the pilgrim leaves the familiar for the strange, leaves the known for the unknown. The next stage of pilgrimage is *The Pilgrim's Way*, or *Crossing the Threshold*. Pilgrims move from ordinary time and space into sacred time and sacred space, where no encounter is without meaning. Once over the threshold, the pilgrim enters the stage of *The Labyrinth*, or *transformation*. This is the heart of the pilgrimage and always involves an element of inner conflict or struggle. For the pilgrim, the traveler with a deep purpose, this is the moment of truth, when the search for God takes you to a place that pierces your heart. The sixth stage is *The Arrival*, the ecstatic moment of receiving the response to the carried intention. The last and final stage of the pilgrimage is *Reincorporation* or *Bringing Back the Boon*. The pilgrim leaves in order to return and bring home the insights, the inspirations, the story of the journey.[5] It is this *story* that is the ultimate aim of the quest as it is what provides us the wisdom and the power to serve others.

The greatest challenge for the returned pilgrim is to learn how to carry over the quality of the journey into your everyday life. For only then shall we know that the end of our explorations, as T.S. Eliot wrote,

We shall not cease from exploration, and the end of all our exploring will be to arrive where we started and know the place for the first time.

PILGRIMAGE: THE LONGING

You are what your deep driving desire is.
-Brihaduranya-ha Upanishad

We all go about the business of our lives, busyness consumes us and rarely do we have a moment to sit, to listen, to breath. And then one day we are awakened to a feeling of deep disturbance-something vital is missing in life. And out of this absence a question begins to emerge. This question looms and feels too big for the typical, daily answer sources. This question seems to call out to a distant sanctuary, a distant holy site that houses the answer. The longing to engage in the ritual act of pilgrimage begins to take shape. The hunger to feed the emptiness is the soul's need for meaning and to find that we must touch and feel these sources of inspiration with our own hands. In turn, we are touched and transformed. It is time to go, immediately.

Isn't it time that your drifting was consecrated into pilgrimage? You have a mission. You are needed. The road that leads to nowhere has to be abandoned....It is a road for joyful pilgrims intent on the recovery of passion.
-Alan Jones

PILGRIMAGE: THE LONGING

What is your life story up to this point? What themes are woven through your years? Do you discern a pattern in the sacred story you are living? These are questions that require the presence of the Spirit-The One who has been with you since the beginning and who can remind you of your authentic expressions. Also, where your heart wanders during those chambered moments will show you the direction of your true longing.

May the lovers of God who went before you, whose devotion to Christ helped make a path for you, grace the way ahead of you with their company and good cheer.
-Jan Richardson

PILGRIMAGE: THE CALLING

Your life is calling you to leave your home, to pack your bags and leave your comforts behind. Your spirit needs you to listen, to really begin listening for the reason behind this journey. It is time to acknowledge your surrender to the Spirit, who will "lead you into unpredictable adventures of the soul."[6] One of the most challenging aspects of responding to this call is the inevitability of *change*: one leaves home only to come back and find *it* a changed place. However, it isn't home that is different, it is you. The prospect of removing our familiar life structures can leave one feeling excitement and dread. Elizabeth Canham further clarifies this tension with these words:

The invitation of God creates resistance because it is a call to change and vulnerability and we have a basic urge to avoid both. Our desire for structures and our fear of chaos play a significant part in our reactions to the possibility of moving on and of relating in new ways. When the call comes, however, it is important to let go of our current perceptions and expectations, or we may fall into the sin of idolatry through our unwillingness to relinquish our current image of the Lord. At the same time we are attracted, drawn irresistibly into a "yes" response despite ourselves.[7]

If you want to travel with the heart of a pilgrim, you need to prepare for your journey. And as always, this requires you to listen. Author and pilgrimage-taker Phil Cousineau talks about "listening to the pilgrim mood in you, to the one who wants to explore the heart and soul of the land you are about to visit."

PILGRIMAGE: THE CALLING

One of Cousineau's methods of "calling" his journey closer to him is to find myths, short stories, poetry and sacred writings about the pilgrimage site. This helps to create the necessary inner adjustment to travel with a pilgrim's heart and a pilgrim's ear.

What has called you to this journey? What is it about Iona that strengthens the 'pilgrim mood' in you?

_____
_____
_____
_____
_____
_____
_____
_____
_____
_____

With the drawing of this Love and the voice of this Calling
we shall not cease from exploration,
and the end of all our exploring
will be to arrive where we started
And know the place for the first time.
-T. S. Eliot in Four Quartets

PILGRIMAGE: THE DEPARTURE/SEPARATION

*God be in my head,
And in my understanding;*

*God be in my eyes,
And in my looking;*

*God be in my mouth,
And in my speaking;*

*God be in my heart,
And in my thinking;*

*God be at my end,
And at my departing.*
-The Sarum Primer

Through preparing your heart for this time apart, an *intention* for the trip will begin to emerge. This intention-or question- will be what you carry with you and what provides the deep meaning of the journey. For medieval pilgrims, the sacred road had a multitude of meanings. For many, they hoped to come in contact with a saint's venerated relics in order to experience healing. Others longed for self-purification, believing in the catharsis of an arduous journey and the merits of constant prayer.[8] For modern day pilgrims, the hardships of the road become a metaphor for the wilderness, a place to where the Spirit calls us so to rely on God alone. And while we may still journey for the sake of healing wounds, it might be more common today to hold a dire question before God; questions related to the future, gifts and calling, vocation and significant life choices are meaningful intentions.

The declaration of intent is not a trivial thing. With it, the pilgrim is saying, "I want to touch and be touched by something holy. After this experience, my life will be different. I will be different. Because I have taken this pilgrimage, I will feel more connected with myself, with others, and with the holy and creative source of life." Each pilgrim's intent is personalized, but it will have these universal features.[9] By declaring your intention for this pilgrimage, you are proclaiming the purpose as sacred. From now on, there is no such thing as a neutral act or meaningless day. The daily contemplations surrounding your intention will begin to align you with God and center your journey.

PILGRIMAGE:
THE DEPARTURE/SEPARATION

Before you depart, it is essential to participate in leave-taking rituals. These separation rituals mark for yourself the place from where you are departing; they represent your current state of mind, your current situations, and your questions. They also prepare you to cross a threshold from the known to the unknown. An example of a leave-taking ritual is a community dinner where you would share with your closest friends and family the intention behind your pilgrimage and to state the hopes and fears of the journey. You might also choose to light candles as you pack as a way of acknowledging the sacred nature of this trip. *Imagine* all the different ways you can prepare for your upcoming journey. Rituals vocalize your openness to being touched and changed by a power that is holy and transcendent.[10]

Poet and author, John O'Donohue, speaks about our collective need to recognize thresholds in life with rituals and blessings. Life is a journey and ultimately the best metaphorical example of a pilgrimage. We cross thresholds throughout our life, but without the sense of the sacred in these crossings, they can become meaningless, disheartened stages. We engage the practice of pilgrimage, with the declaration of intention and leave-taking rituals, to acknowledge our surrender to the Spirit, and to "reawaken our capacity for blessing." O'Donohue shares with us,

A threshold is a significant frontier where experience banks up; there is intense concrescence. It is a place of great transformation. Some of the most powerful thresholds divide

PILGRIMAGE:
THE DEPARTURE/SEPARATION

worlds from each other; life in the womb from birth, childhood from adolescence, adulthood from middle age, old age from death. And on each side there is a different geography of feelings, thinking, and being. The crossing of a threshold is in effect a rite of passage. Our culture has little to offer us for our crossings. Never was there such talk of communication or such technology to facilitate it. Yet at the heart of our newfound wealth and progress there is a gaping emptiness, and we are haunted by loneliness. While we seem to have progressed to become experts in so many things— multiplying and acquiring stuff we neither need nor truly want—we have unlearned the grace of presence and belonging. With the demise of religion, many people are left stranded in a chasm of emptiness and doubt; without rituals to recognize, celebrate, or negotiate the vital thresholds of people's lives, the key crossings pass by, undistinguished from the mundane, everyday rituals of life. This is where we need to retrieve and reawaken our capacity for blessing. If we approach our decisive thresholds with reverence and attention, the crossing will bring us more than we could ever have hoped for. This is where blessing invokes and awakens every gift the crossing has to offer. In our present ritual poverty, the Celtic tradition has much to offer us.[11]

Your statement of intent and leave-taking rituals that allow you to declare your hopes and fears are a part of the separation stage of pilgrimage. The sacred journey is not just about leaving the ordinary rhythms and places of life. The process is much more and involves stages of moving from ordinary space into sacred space and then back again. The stages of

PILGRIMAGE:
THE DEPARTURE/SEPARATION

pilgrimage-as of any life threshold-are important because they are more about what occurs within the pilgrim than about the physical process of leaving and returning home.[12]

Is an intention forming within you? Why do you feel you are taking this pilgrimage?

PILGRIMAGE: THE PILGRIM'S WAY/ CROSSING THE THRESHOLD

How wonderful it is to walk with God along the road which holy men have trod.
-Theodore H. Kitching

The purpose of the pilgrimage is to ultimately make life more meaningful. It is regarded as the universal quest for the self. Though the form of the path changes, one element remains the same: renewal of the soul. The essence of the sacred way is "tracing a sacred route of tests and trials, ordeals and obstacles, to arrive at a holy place and attempt to fathom the secrets of its power."[13] Once again, the act of listening is emphasized here. The way of the pilgrim is one of an inner-quiet, an inner ear tuned to the subtle sounds of the Spirit while on the sacred road.

Once the acts of intention and attention are completed, the pilgrim is ready to cross the *threshold*. The threshold is more than an architectural detail; it is a mythological image that evokes the spirit of resistance we must pass through on our journey from all we've known to all that is unknown. It is the first step toward renewal.[14] Once on the other side, pilgrims move from ordinary time and space into sacred time and sacred space. In this reality, the meanings we associate with our normal everyday experiences are turned upside down. The structures we use to define who we are in ordinary life become irrelevant. Pilgrim space has no regard for class, race, or social/economic standing. There are no more random run-ins with strangers; there are no more lucky or misfortunate moments. In sacred travel, every experience is uncanny; every contact attests to some greater plan. No encounter is without meaning. There are signs everywhere, if only we learn how to read them. Peculiar people turn into much-needed messengers. "From now," advised Epictetus, "practice

PILGRIMAGE:
THE PILGRIM'S WAY/
CROSSING THE THRESHOLD

saying to everything that appears unpleasant: 'you are just an appearance and by no means what you appear to be.'" Use the powers of your sacred imagination, the old Roman sage is saying. See behind the veil of things. Listen to the message between every spoken word. Everything matters along the road, but what matters deeply is what is invisible and must be seen with the inner eye.[15]

If the journey you have chosen is indeed a pilgrimage, a soulful journey, it will be rigorous. Ancient wisdom suggests if you aren't trembling as you approach the sacred, it isn't the real thing. The sacred, in its various guises as holy ground, art, or knowledge, evokes emotion and commotion.
-Phil Cousineau

Wherever God has called us to be at this moment is the place for us to become mystics and prophets. We do this by simply paying attention and asking ourselves, "What does this mean to me? What do I see and what must I say, by my life as well as my lips, as a result of this seeing?"[16]

What encounters stand out in your mind as one's with greater meaning in the context of pilgrimage?

_____
_____
_____
_____
_____
_____
_____

When the path is simple, peace.

When the way is complicated, peace.

May Christ not only show you the way, but also be the way you travel: way of blessing, way of peace.
-Jan Richardson

PILGRIMAGE: THE LABYRINTH/ TRANSFORMATION

*Lord of every new day
when the road ahead is
totally scary
or far too comfortable,
reveal your life-giving waymarks,
so that having made them our own,
we travel on with risk,
vulnerability,
vision,
awareness,
passion,
struggle,
energy
and compassion as our constant companions.
-Peter Millar*

The image of the labyrinth is an ancient symbol for the meandering path of the soul that goes from light into darkness and emerges once again into light. The soul emanates transformed. This darkness (the wilderness) is the heart of the pilgrimage and always involves an element of inner conflict or struggle. It is the time spent within the wilderness where you meet your fears and confront them-where you come up against whatever prevents you from hearing the voice of God or living a life of compassion and generosity.[17]

The answer to the pilgrim's intention is at the heart of the journey. One cannot simply arrive at that place; the answers to the heart do not answer to immediacy. Instead, we wonder, weave and walk in circumambulation-both literally and metaphorically. It is the pilgrim's steady and winding movements that lead toward the sacred center. The labyrinth is meant to be a defense; built to guard a center, a treasure, a meaning. Entering it can be a rite of initiation. And entering it can mean engaging the darkness that also surrounds the center as a means of protection. The dark stretch of the pilgrimage, however, can also be the most illuminating. Our most secret and raw places are kept in the dark recesses of our heart. To truly get to the center, to the heart of our journey, we must go into these dark places, knowing that God is our Guide and our Light. For the pilgrim, the traveler with a deep purpose, this is the moment of truth, when the search for the *real* takes you to a place that pierces your heart.[18]

PILGRIMAGE: THE LABYRINTH/ TRANSFORMATION

Phil Cousineau straightforwardly outlines ordeals the journey itself offers as means of initiating the labyrinth stage:

For the pilgrim traveling a great distance and at great personal expense, the image of a path coiling into a labyrinth as the destination nears is a powerful one. Fear, sacrifice, confusion, betrayal, theft, even death are the invariables travelers are loath to think about. The sheer physical exertion of the thousand-mile walk to a saint's tomb can evoke strong emotions of resentment and doubt; the loss of money, passport, or a travel companion can threaten a long-planned journey. You may have been given wrong directions, or perhaps deliberately entrapped by con artists. Your baggage may have been misdirected and not returned to you for a week. You may feel savaged with disappointments about the people with whom you are fated to travel on a group pilgrimage. Unaccustomed loneliness, unfamiliar food, unexpectedly kitschy architecture at the shrine you have dreamed of visiting all your life—all these disappointments can result in the confusion, frustration, and chaos that have been symbolized for centuries in the image of the labyrinth.[19]

Inevitably darkness and dismay will descend on your journey. Cousineau goes on to say that "patience, silence, trust, and faith are venerable qualities of the pilgrim, but more important is the practice of them."[20] They become the light that will illuminate the darkness and reveal that which is at your sacred center.

PILGRIMAGE: THE LABYRINTH/ TRANSFORMATION

That you will let yourself be lost
from time to time
in the labyrinth of the Word.
That you may, for awhile,
empty yourself of all the words you know,
that Christ the living Word
will find you
and fill you
with his wisdom.
That he will write himself anew
across the pages of your life.
-*Jan Richardson*

How will you answer the voice who asks you now to describe what you are enduring halfway through your pilgrimage? For every time we move toward a significant goal, the world has a tendency to throw terrific obstacles in our way.
-*P. Cousineau*

_____
_____
_____
_____
_____
_____
_____
_____
_____

PILGRIMAGE: THE LABYRINTH/ TRANSFORMATION

Midway on our life's journey, I found myself
    In dark woods, the right road lost. To tell
    About those woods is hard-so tangled and rough
And savage that thinking of it now, I feel
    The old fear stirring: death is hardly more bitter.
    And yet, to treat the good I found their as well
I'll tell what i saw....
-from THE INFERNO OF DANTE, Robert Pinsky, trans.[21]

Imagine that your task in the labyrinth is to find the center. When in doubt, remember your original intention for the journey; recall your purpose; reinstate your vow; rekindle your fire by doing something passionate; rediscover the thread that led you to your pilgrimage in the first place. Remember the risks you took, the physical and spiritual dangers you've encountered, the financial and spiritual sacrifices you've made, were to rediscover what is most sacred in your life.
-P. Cousineau

PILGRIMAGE: ARRIVAL

The sun *will* rise on the day that brings you physically to the destination of the pilgrimage. Your mind and emotions will be buzzing with excitement; your task is to feel the *thrill* of completing your pilgrimage to this stage. There is deep joy to having arrived yet some of the most focused practices of pilgrimage need to be maintained for the journey to remain in focus. The disciplines of *listening* and seeing with the heart of a pilgrim are essential now at the stage of *arrival*.

Prepare for the destination by restating the fundamental question in your heart and mind, your *intention*. Hold this in thought and prayer as you ready yourself for the day. It would also be helpful to meditate on Scripture, journal, and read poetry-all actions that will focus your energies at the momentous arrival to your journey's end. Prepare to practice the spirit of mindfulness. Ritualize each act as you approach the destination, remembering that there is no such thing "as a throwaway gesture or a neutral thought [as] the vey act of pilgrimage magnetizes each stage of the journey."[22] This might be done by silently reciting a short blessing or prayer during the final stages of the journey leading to the sacred end. Perhaps a chant from a hymnbook, or the repetition of a mantra would help ritualize the moments before arrival. Whatever is holy to you, whatever brings you peace is what should be practiced at this stage of pilgrimage.

PILGRIMAGE:ARRIVAL

Phil Cousineau shares these methods of preparation for the day of arrival:

On the morning of the day of your arrival at the sacred site that was the goal of your journey, recall what the prophecies have said in your dreams, in the sacred books you read to prepare for this auspicious moment. Try to see everything around you at this moment as portentous—the birdsong outside your window, the on the [trees], the way the clouds have formed over the mountains in the distance. Sit in bed a few extra minutes with your eyes closed. You have risen earlier than usual, from anticipation. Pay close attention to any dreams still frothing on the surface of your mind. Is there something welling up inside you that has flamed into dream? Before you do anything else, read a few lines from a book you consider spiritually appropriate for your visit....[23]

Reflect on what the equivalents of a gracious arrival are for you. The way of the pilgrim is not to *take*, like that of a typical tourist. Instead, the pilgrim thoughtfully and intentionally leaves something of value behind. This gesture underscores the gratitude that is felt for the pilgrimage and journey's end. You might think of lighting a candle in honor of your intention, or write down something in your journal that you want your grandchildren to remember you by. Leave behind an offering or a trinket that represents what you discovered at your sacred center.

PILGRIMAGE: ARRIVAL

You have arrived. Your pilgrimage began long ago as the yearning to go relentlessly etched itself onto your heart. Because of, and out of your preparation, you have expectantly traveled toward this wisdom site with hands to the One who is the origin of all things, including both questions...and answers. The Holy Presence awaits you and invites, if not demands, you pay attention. Everything about this journey has called you ultimately heed the sacred source of your life. You have arrived. What will you receive? What will you give. For we know that it is only when we give that we truly receive. What is this vital thing that you alone can offer up in this space, at this time?

PILGRIMAGE: REINCORPORATION/ BRINGING BACK THE BOON

The one thing the pilgrim returns home with is *wisdom* and the responsibility to share the truth gleaned from the profound pilgrimage. The story that we bring back from our journeys is the boon. There is a universal code of sorts, which requires the pilgrim to "share whatever wisdom you've been blessed with on your journey with those who are about to set out on their own journey."[24] The challenge and bitter truth of coming home from a pilgrimage is that we soon learn that what is a pearl to us is mere pennies to others. How can we even begin to describe the depths to which our soul has traveled? Ultimately, our changed life must tell the story of our journey; no picture slide show or souvenir will scratch the surface of the truth found at the sacred center.

In Joseph Campbell's popular book of essays *Myths to Live By*, he described something pertinent to our theme of sacred journeys: "The ultimate air of the quest if one is to return, must be neither release nor ecstasy for oneself, but the wisdom and the power to serve others." This parallels the belief of the ancient wisdom teachers that the ultimate answer to the sorrows of the world is the boon of increased self-knowledge.[25] Interestingly enough, this responsibility resonates with Frederick Buechner's definition of vocation as "the place where your deep gladness and the world's deep hunger meet." It seems clear that the great value of a pilgrimage is to return with a knowledge of self that will enable one to engage the world's needs in an authentic and passionate way. Because of the journey to the sacred center, and the perils

PILGRIMAGE: REINCORPORATION/ BRINGING BACK THE BOON

experienced to get there, you are transformed. And because you have changed, so will your home. You have encountered the Holy-experienced God in a fresh new way-and as a result of your epiphany and your struggle, you will not relate to your world or those in it as you did before.[26] Your challenge is to now live into the new edges of your life, inhabiting the new spaces created by pushing through the trails of your inner-soul landscape. These are the places where dynamic opportunities lay for you to share your wisdom and bring back the boon of your journey.

Set up waymarks for yourself,
Make yourself guideposts:
Consider well the highway,
The road by which you went.
Jeremiah 31:21

In the fire of revelation,
in the clarity of illumination,
in the shadows of mystery,
in the silence of prayer,
may the Word of God
inscribe itself on your soul
and illumine your way.
-Jan Richardson

*Blessed are those who
know their need,
for theirs is the
grace of heaven.
-Matthew 5:3*

WAYMARKER: FLYING

We begin our pilgrimage to Iona, Scotland with a flight across the world. Charles Lindbergh's flight in May 1927 ushered in the era of long-distance air line routes, ones that span the world today. These Trans-Atlantic flights seem almost routine as we sit in the back of an air-conditioned Boeing or an Airbus. This relatively new technology has made the world and it's various communities accessible with relative ease. We acknowledge that prior to air travel, it would have taken us almost three months to travel to Scotland across the Atlantic Ocean, an amount of time that would likely make this pilgrimage next to impossible.

Today, with seeming ease and entitlement, we simply fly over this vast body of water, possibly never even seeing and appreciating its vastness and imperative role in our life on earth. And yet these waters teem with creatures and are essential to life as we know it on this planet. Life comes from water! The Psalmist, in Psalm 104, details the many wondrous acts of God's provision using water images, referencing the beginning of creation of the earth when it was set on its foundations and covered "with the deep as with a garment' (104:6). Consistent with other ancient creation traditions, Genesis understands water as the basis of all creation. Water is understood as the source of all life, a gift from God for the sustenance of all creation.

Water flows over these hands. May I use them skillfully to preserve our precious planet.
-Thich Nhat Hanh

Tell me, what is it you plan to do with your one wild and precious life?
-Mary Oliver

WAYMARKER: FLYING

Praise the Lord from the earth, you sea creatures and all deeps.
Psalm 148:7

Blessed with easily accessible water, we in the Western world often forget that water is a God-given gift. Without water, we, and the rest of God's beloved creation, would not have life. Jesus references himself as the *source* of living water in John's Gospel. How can the living water help us to respond to the real needs of God's beloved creation for reliable sources, of clean, fresh water? Can we also look to the *living* water as a way to understand how we are to live in right relationship with our *physical* waters?[27]

Psalm 42 describes the presence of God as enveloping waves and billows; how do you feel God's encompassing presence already on this journey? What other watery images and symbols come to mind when you think of God's provisions for yourself, this pilgrimage and others?

WAYMARKER:FLYING

Bless the Lord, O my soul.
O Lord my God, you are very great.
You are clothed with honor and majesty,
wrapped in light as with a garment.
You stretch out the heavens like a tent,
you set the beams of your chambers
on the waters,
you make the clouds your chariot,
you ride on the wings of the wind,
you make the winds your messengers....
-Psalm 104:1-4

All of creation has its origin in water-the earth itself came out of the waters. In the first chapter of Genesis, God separates the waters above from the waters below, and then creates the earth out of the waters. Hovering, brooding, blowing over these teeming waters was the Spirit, present and co-creator with God in the very beginning. The Spirit of God in Genesis 1 is sometimes translated as 'wind.' The Celtic tradition saw her as a great bird poised over the waters of chaos to bring creation to birth; her breath, the wind, "fertilizing the waters," drawing forth hidden life forms "into visible forms and corporeal beauties."[28]

WAYMARKER: FLYING

Life came out of the waters, drawn forth from the Wind of God, Yahweh's very breath. Mystics say that the forgotten pronunciation of the name of God is *Yah* on the whispered in-breath and *Weh* on the whispered out-breath. Thus the whole name for God is formed by a single cycle of the breath, the awesome mystery of God's name not separate from the very mystery of breathing.

Consider the words of Psalm 104, "You ride on the wings of the wind." Allow images of the wind to be recalled within you. As you reflect on these words and mental pictures, find rhythm in your breath; listen for the *Yah* and *Wey* in your breathing. Allow this to remind you that in your very breath you are in communion with the Spirit, the Wind of God, who dwells at the heart of your life and who is guiding you on this pilgrimage.

WAYMARKER:FLYING

Looking through white, pillowed cloud
below to warm, green quilt of land-
challenged am I to remain present,
above-in the sky.
My mind hastens to the heather,
to home.
Here requires my heart's attention.
Present must I be in the clouds.
-Mary A. DeJong

Bless to me O God
My soul that comes from on high.
Bless to me O God
My body that is of earth.
Bless to me O God
Each thing my eye sees
Each sound my ear hears.
Bless to me O God
Each scent that goes to my nostrils
Each taste that goes to my lips
Each ray that guides my way.
-J. Philip Newell

WAYMARKER: FLYING

Be Thou a smooth way before me,
Be Thou a guiding star above me,
Be Thou a keen eye behind me,
This day, this night, for ever.
I am weary, and I am forlorn,
Lead Thou me to the land of the angels;
Methinks it were time I went for a space
To the court of Christ, to the peace of heaven;
If only Thou, O God of life,
Be at peace with me, be my support,
Be to me as a star, be to me as a helm,
From my lying down in peace to my rising anew.
-*Carmina Gadelica, I, 171*

Instructions For Wayfarers
They will declare: Every journey has been taken.
You shall respond: I have not been to see myself.
They will insist: Everything has been spoken.
You shall reply: I have not had my say.

They will tell you: Everything has been done.
You shall reply: My way is not complete.

You are warned: Any way is long, any way is hard.
Fear not. You are the gate – you, the gatekeeper.
And you shall go through and on . . .
—Alexandros Evangelou Xenopouloudakis, *Third Wish*
Robert Fulghum, 2006

WAYMARKER:GLASGOW-BUS

In Kathleen Norris's book, *Dakota: A Spiritual Geography*, she writes about living in New York and then moving to rural South Dakota where her family was rooted: "I am conscious of carrying a Plains silence within me into cities, and of carrying my city experiences back to the Plains so that they may be absorbed again back into silence, the fruitful silence that produces poems and essays."

Isn't that something of what each of us wants? To be able to experience the mutual creativity that is exchanged between City and Nature? Both call to us and our gifts and don't need to be seen as mutually exclusive of one another. As one thinks about their future and where they want to live and work, often the City/Rural is seen as an either/or. We are being invited to move from the 'city' hustle and bustle of our every day lives, into the silence of nature and our inner spirit and back again. The invitation is to find the serene silence even in the City.

Another way of reflecting on this dynamic is by looking at both solitude and community. Consider the example of the beginning of Jesus' Galilean ministry as described in the Gospel of Mark's first chapter. We see here that Jesus was a person compassionately engaged with the needs of people in the city and lived out his 'vocation' with clarity and great sense of purpose. It is significant to note that he honored the need to take time out for silence and communion with God, and regularly did so in wilderness spaces. Gordon T. Smith, in Courage and Calling (Inter Varsity Press, 1999), states, "Solitude is essential for vocational clarity and integrity because it is in solitude that we are enabled to sustain a connection, a relationship, with the one who has called us."

Who am I and who has God called me to be?

WAYMARKER: GLASGOW-BUS

May you listen into the work and around it; may you listen within it, behind and beneath it. May you let your true work lead you into the places that only it knows.
-Jan Richardson

Most of us live in densely populated urban areas where the needs of the City are great. If indeed solitude is necessary to sustain a life of purpose and compassion how do you intend to incorporate this practice into your life?

WAYMARKER: GLASGOW-BUS

In the histories of nations, innovations in technology have sometimes occurred at such a rapid pace that the era becomes known as an industrial revolution. This occurred in North America in the late 1800's and early 1900's. Industrial developments moved the country from a largely rural population that made its livelihood almost entirely from agriculture to a town-centered society that was increasingly engaged in factory manufacturing. This movement had both positive and negative effects on people. More, better, and inexpensive goods, as well as transportation and communication were possible. On the other hand, industry also brought pollution, poverty, child labor issues, and enormous amounts of people to cities.

While modern cities are increasingly improving their carbon footprint through various sustainable programs and building techniques, we still see a lot of poverty and deprivation in urban centers. What needs of the City move you towards compassion and action?

We become human only when we dedicate ourselves to someone in greater need, only when we choose to use our lives for others to bring about a better world.
–Cesar Chavez

_____

_____

_____

_____

_____

_____

_____

_____

_____

_____

WAYMARKER: GLASGOW-BUS

There is no place that humans have left untouched; and there is no place that the wild does not, in some small way, proclaim itself.
-Lyanda Lynn Haupt

O Christ of the poor and the yearning
Kindle in my heart within
A flame of love for my neighbor,
For my foe, for my friend,
for my kindred all.
From the humblest thing that lives
To the name that is highest of all
Kindle in my heart within a flame of love.
-J. Philip Newell

The Journey Prayer
God, bless to me this day,
God, bless to me this night;
Bless, O bless, Thou God of grace,
Each day and hour of my life;
Bless, O bless, Thou God of grace,
Each day and hour of my life.

God, bless the pathway on which I go,
God, bless the earth that is beneath my sole;
Bless, O God, and give to me Thy love,
O God of gods, bless my rest and my repose;
Bless, O God, and give to me Thy love,
And bless, O God of gods, my repose.
-Carmina Gadelica, III, 179

WAYMARKER: THE RAIL

As the train departs Queen Street Station, there is a sense you are ever the more committed to this pilgrimage journey. Perhaps for the first time, you feel you are able to breath a sigh of relief; you've made it to Scotland, you navigated a new urban center and now you, and your bags, are secure for the time being. You may be compelled to breathe a little easier and put your feet up. Enjoy this part of the journey, which takes you along the world-famous West Highland Line.

This "Iron Road to the Isles" is on the most scenic railway lines in Britain, linking the ports of Mallaig and Oban on the west coast of Scotland to Glasgow. The line was voted the top rail journey in the world by readers of independent travel magazine Wanderlust in 2009, ahead of the iconic Trans-Siberian and the Cuzco to Machu Picchu line in Peru.[29]

This part of the journey will begin to familiarize you with the Scottish landscape and the local people. Gaze out the window and take in the new territory; listen to and enjoy the musical language of the Scottish brogue about you. Savor the moment of knowing that you are well on your way to Iona.

Does the road wind uphill all the way?
Yes, to the very end.
Will the journey take the whole long day?
From morn to night, my friend.
-Christina Rossetti, 1867

WAYMARKER: THE RAIL

"Pilgrims are persons in motion-passing through territories not their own-seeking something we might call contemplation, or perhaps the word clarity will do as well, a goal to which only the Spirit's compass points the way."
–Richard Niebuhr

A pilgrim way is a meeting place between history, culture, nature and you. A pilgrim way is a human way, connecting you and fellow human being in the past, present and future— with spiritual inspiration reverberating through it all.
-Pilgrimage to Nidaros

We leave the urban centers and travel through suburbs into the countryside. What does this transition feel like to you?

_____

_____

_____

_____

The train as metaphor has existed as long as the tracks themselves. The railroad has represented civilization, progress, and industry. It has been seen as the visage of opportunity with the midnight whistle blow being one of the most compelling beckoning calls of the twentieth century.
List the metaphors that come to mind for you when you reflect on the image of the train and railroad and how they relate to your modern-day pilgrimage.

_____

_____

_____

_____

WAYMARKER: THE RAIL

This day and this night
may I know O God
The deep peace
of the running wave
The deep peace
of the flowing air
The deep peace
of the quiet earth
The deep peace
of the shining stars
The deep peace
of the Son of Peace.
-*Carmina Gadelica*

I feel Thy presence
in this landscape
which draws my
heart so close to Thee.
-*Hazrat Inayat Khan*

May time spiral well for you,
leading you around
and around yet again
to the landscapes where remembering
offers redemption and grace.
-*Jan Richardson*

WAYMARKER: ISLE OF MULL FERRY

Listen to the cries of the sea gulls; what do their calls stir in you as they fly over the wavy waters?

Oban is the major departure point for ferries to the Hebrides and it remains the largest port in North West Scotland. The Mull ferry, aptly named the Isle of Mull was built in 1988 at Port Glasgow on the Clyde. She is designed to accommodate up to 80 cars and up to 972 passengers, thus providing for the heavy amount of pedestrian pilgrims going to Mull en route to Iona. As you depart the port, draw your attention to the wonderful views of Oban laid out around its natural amphitheatre and topped off by McCaig's Tower, with its looming hilltop presence. Oban appears to be releasing her embrace of you, sending you further on your pilgrimage. Enjoy this part of the journey from the promenade decks as the height of the ferry allows for sweeping views of the inlets and isles in passage to the Isle of Mull.

The features of this part of the journey are spectacular but none may be as evocative in all of Scotland than that of Duart Castle back dropped by Mull's mountains. This stronghold resisted attacks from marauders and Vikings for hundreds of years.[30]

As you look upon this ancient ruin, do you feel you need protection from something on this journey?
Remember that God is your stronghold! Surround yourself in God's strength! Rejoice that you have come this far!

_____

_____

_____

WAYMARKER:
ISLE OF MULL FERRY

"Dear Lord, today I thought of the words of Vincent van Gogh: 'It is true there is an ebb and flow, but the sea remains the sea.' You are the sea. Although I experience many ups and downs in my emotions and often feel great shifts and changes in my inner life, you remain the same. Your sameness is not the sameness of a rock, but the sameness of a faithful lover. Out of your love I came to life; by your love I am sustained, and to your love I am always called back. O, Lord, sea of love and goodness, let me not fear too much the storms and winds of my daily life, and let me know that There is ebb and flow but that the sea remains the sea." Amen.
-Henri Nouwen

On the day you were born
the Moon pulled on the ocean below,
and, wave by wave,
a rising tide washed the beaches clean
for your footprints
while far out at sea
clouds swelled with water drops,
sailed to shore on a wind,
and rained you a welcome
across the Earth's green lands.
-Debra Fraisier, On the Day You Were Born (1991)

The sea is God's, for God made it, and the dry land, which God's hands have formed.
Psalm 95:5

WAYMARKER: ISLE OF MULL FERRY

When the poor and needy seek water, and there is none, and their tongue is parched with thirst, I the Lord will answer them, I the God of Israel will not forsake them. I will open rivers on the bare heights, and fountains in the midst of the valleys; I will make the wilderness a pool of water, and the dry land springs of water.
Isaiah 41:17-18

Examine the form of the sea-its contours, its colors, its movements, its shape. The sea's flowing waters respond to the lunar pull of the moon. There is a created design in this significant relationship, which illuminates the dynamic the pilgrim experiences between the call and the journey towards the destination. And in this tenuous tidal ebb and flow, we remember to listen and practice attention to the community of creation all around us.

Listen to the waters.

_____

_____

_____

_____

Let the waters wash away any indifference you have, any despair you feel, any fear which clouds your vision. And let it symbolize the outpouring of the Holy Spirit upon a transformed people. Let it remind us of the thirst of the earth and the thirst of the people in many parts of the world who live parched lives. Let it remind us of the dream of children to dance and bathe and drink clean water. Let it remind us of the promise of scripture that streams will break forth in the desert, and that the river of the water of death will be replaced by the river of the water of life.
-Janet Parker

WAYMARKER:
ISLE OF MULL FERRY

The mountaineer and the fisherman and the shepherd
of the Isles live their lives in lonely places, and the
winds and waves bear to them messages from the unknown
beyond.
-Wilkie

The Ocean Blessing

Carry us over the surface of the sea,
Carry us safely to a haven of peace,
Bless our boatmen and our boat,
Bless our anchors and our oars,
Each stay and halyard and traveler,
Our mainsails to our tall masts
Keep, O King of the elements, in their place
That we may return home in peace.
-Anonymous (found taped to a wall in the Fionnphort Ferry Terminal)

WAYMARKER:
ISLE OF MULL FERRY

The Pilot Psalm

The Lord is my Pilot; I shall not drift.
He lighteth me across the dark waters:
He steereth me in deep channels.
He keepeth my log:
He guideth me by the star of holiness
For his names sake.
Yea though I sail mid the thunder
and tempest of life,
I will dread no danger for Thou art near me:
Thy love and Thy care they shelter me.
Thou preparest a harbour before me
in the homeland of eternity.
Thou anointest the waves
with oil my ship rideth calmly.
Surely sunlight and starlight
shall favour me on the voyage I take:
and I will rest in the port of my God
forever.
-Capt.John H.Roberts – 1874

WAYMARKER: MULL-BUS

The Isle of Mull, or simply Mull, is the second largest island of the Inner Hebrides, the string of maritime islands off the west coast of Scotland. The island's natural, wild beauty is crowned with a mountainous core, the highest peak on the island being Ben More, striking at 3,170 feet (966 meters) above sea level. Mull plays host to a plethora of wildlife including the white tailed eagle, golden eagles, otters and basking sharks found off the coast.

This passage through Mull maintains evidence of the first pilgrimage route pilgrims would've taken to Iona for the past millennium; there are large standing stones on Mull (and other Hebeidrian Islands) that are thought to be way markers to Iona for the ancient traveler.

Imagine coming upon these large monoliths today. Would they strike in you overwhelming anticipation for your pending arrival? What emotions would these monuments conjure?

May the King shield you in the valleys,
May Christ aid you on the mountains.
May Spirit bathe you on the slopes,
In hollow, on hill, on plain, mountain, valley and plain.
-Carmina Gadelica, III, 209

_____
_____
_____
_____
_____
_____
_____
_____
_____
_____

WAYMARKER: MULL-BUS

Come forth into the light of things. Let Nature be your teacher.
–William Wordsworth

There is no plant in the ground
But tells of your beauty, O Christ.
There is no creature on the earth,
there is no life in the sea,
But proclaims your goodness.
There is no bird on the wing,
there is no star in the sky,
There is nothing beneath the sun
but is full of your blessing.
Lighten my understanding
of your presence all around, O Christ.
Kindle my will
to be caring for Creation.
-J. Philip Newell

Speak to me, Lord, give me Your peace.
Show me the way to go.
I need Your love, I need Your strength,
all of my needs you know.

Be by my side, be in my heart.
Be in my every prayer.
Filling my life, filling my soul,
all of the time be there…

Give me Your love,
give me Your peace….
-Ros Robertson

WAYMARKER: MULL-BUS

Mull's vast open space is a geography formed by an earlier ice age. This island's fascinating geology is well preserved in volcanic formation, which has been shaped by glacial erosion. Mull has some very rare rock types and well preserved volcanic formations. These attract geologists from all over the world and it is these rock structures underneath the surface that make Mull one of the most attractive islands in the Hebrides. The island's geology gives Mull its varied and beautiful scenery.

As we drive through this rugged terrain, what is forming you? What is forming in you right now?

How will you answer the voice who asks you now to describe what you are enduring half way through your pilgrimage?
-Phil Cousineau

WAYMARKER: MULL-BUS

God of the Twisting Path, God of the Turning Spiral, God of Revelation, God of Infinite Mystery; may this God enfold and entwine you in every step.
-St. Brigid

Like a mother holding her child
you comfort me.
As old as the mountains,
as new as the rain,
you are constant and strong,
peaceful and powerful.
Hide me in the stillness of your pools,
nurture me with your abundant life.
Carry me along your gentle flow,
bear me up through your fierce rapids.
Hold me in your memory,
let my heart never forget you.
-Robert Hamma

The bus ride through the Isle of Mull is a sensory experience. Not only are you viewing amazing vistas, but your body is being jolted and jerked by the bus' starts and stops. These Scottish single lane roads are not for the faint of heart. See the bus' circumnavigation as a kind of labyrinth, twisting and turning, stirring both anticipation and trepidation.

As the bus swerves and turns through this wild landscape, reflect on what might be jarring your inner journey on the pilgrimage thus far.

_____

_____

_____

_____

WAYMARKER: MULL-BUS

You make springs gush forth in the valleys; they flow between the hills, giving drink to every wild animal; the wild asses quench their thirst. By the streams the birds of the air have their habitation; they sing among the branches. From your lofty abode you water the mountains; the earth is satisfied with the fruit of your work.
Psalm 104: 10-13

Those who contemplate the beauty of the earth find reserves of strength that will endure as long as life lasts.
-*Rachel Carson*

If you love it enough anything will talk to you.
-George Washington Carver

WAYMARKER: MULL-BUS

It is not the language of painters but the language of nature which one should listen to...the feeling for the things themselves, for reality is more important than the feeling for pictures.
–Vinvent Van Gogh

Look for roadside streams and ponds-see these of visuals of refreshment. What is refreshing you on your pilgrimage until now?

_____

_____

_____

Take in the vast storehouse of natural beauty in the forests, trees, high hills, and mountaintops. What is Creation saying to you about our Creator? What is our Creator saying to you through this Creation?

_____

_____

_____

The landscape is stitched with ribbons of rock walls, their aesthetic as valued as their purpose. Focus on the function of the rock wall. Look to all the rocks that make up the total piece, the wall/fence. What are the rocks in your life that is creating your function, your vocation? What are the key 'stones' that, when put together, speak to your purpose?

_____

_____

_____

WAYMARKER:IONA-FERRY

You no longer need your imagination. You can cast your guidebooks aside. There is Iona. You are one in an annual company of 250,000 pilgrims who come to this island, making the long journey to this remote and rocky place to find God, peace and restoration. By their nature, pilgrimages collect people from all cultures; you are likely surrounded by many right now. Practice patience. Your time here will be authentically yours. We are reminded by the poet-pilgrim, Basho of the essential role of spirituality in travel: the *inward* experience while traveling outward along roads of the world is of greatest value.

Capture your impressions as you cross the waters to the Isle of Iona, the place of your longing.

> *This is the great moment, when you see, however distant, the goal of your wandering. The thing which has been living in your imagination suddenly becomes a part of the tangible world.*
> –Freya Stark

WAYMARKER:IONA~FERRY

May you discern where to extend a welcome, and where to receive one.

This, then, is the Iona of Columba.
There is the bay where the little, sea-tossed coracle drove ashore. There is the hill-the Hill of Angels-where heavenly visitors shone before him. There is the Sound across which the men of Mull heard vespers sung by hooded monks-heard the Lord's song sung in a strange land. There is the narrow strip of water across which holy men came to take counsel, sinners to do penance, kings to be crowned. The little island speaks with a quiet insistence of its past-for was it not at once the fountain and the fortress of the faith, at once the centre of Celtic learning and of Christian charity?
-*Troup*

In Iona of my heart, Iona of my love,
instead of monk's voice
Shall be lowing of cows;
but ere the world shall come to an end
Iona shall be as it was.
-*Attributed to Columba*

WAYMARKER:IONA-FERRY

A Pilgrim's Companion Psalm
The road home, O God, seems long
and at time is difficult and painful.
Grant me a holy communion, a companionship with others,
as I journey homeward to you.
I live in times of great trial:
an age of change sits at my door.
Without a community with others
I can so easily loose the way,
can be led astray by illusions of holiness,
misguided by my ego's desires.
Open my eyes to your precious gift
of the Church's Communion of Saints.
"Saint" is a name I would never call myself,
but the treasury of my faith
teaches me about my holy birthright,
that I am part of the web of sacred communion,
united me with all other home-bound pilgrims
and with all who now rejoice
at their homecoming in you.
May I feed this day upon the food
of this mystic, holy communion
with those friends and fellow pilgrims
with whom I share this planet Earth,
as well as those saints now fully one with you.
May this awareness of my companion journey

(continued)

WAYMARKER:IONA-FERRY

with all the saints
deepen my life of prayer
and fertilize my faith in you, my Beloved.
By this communion of holy ones
may I be daily challenged
to greater compassion and charity
as I walk the way of the pilgrim.
-*Edward Hays*

Unlike mere travel, a pilgrimage is a journey into the landscape of the soul.
-*Vivienne Hull*

WAYMARKER: IONA-FERRY

'A place of hope',
They say:
And in their thousands
They journey, year by year,
To this tiny island
On the margins of Europ.
Sunswept and windswept,
Yet always deeply
A place of transformation.
A sacred spot on earth:
A pilgrim's place
Of light and shadow,
Energy and challenge.

We need you, Iona.
With your alternative vision,
With your ever-present questions,
Your often uncomfortable silence.

For you are a place of prayer,
Of Christ's abiding:
Weaving a rainbow of meaning
Through the endless busyness of
our days,
Holding together the frayed
threads

Of our fleeting devotion,
Opening a path for healing

WAYMARKER:IONA-FERRY

And for peace.
Not momentary healing
Nor easy faith,
But struggle, commitment,
And an ongoing conversion
Are your gifts for
Our broken yet beautiful lives.
-Peter Millar, An Iona Prayer Book

Thine be the might of river,
Thine b the might of ocean, ...
The might of victory of field.
Thine be the might of fire,...
Thine be the might of element,...
The might of love on high.
-Carmina Gadelica, III, 237

WAYMARKER:HOME AGAIN

It is in going out that we discover what is really going on, both in our inner-heart's landscape and in our physical home places. The journey away from home brings with it fresh perspectives and abilities to see our normal lives with a new sense of discovery and sensitivity. We return with a posture of being newly awakened-tuned in and aware of the Spirit all around us. The daily challenge is to carry over the quality of the journey into everyday life.

We are challenged to live into the deeper understanding of ourselves and our God-given talents and gifts. Because the inner-journey has righted priorities and passions, we embrace the gift of relationships in our lives-loving and respecting those who have been given to us to nurture. We answer the call to do justice, knowing that however we employ our calling that it must somehow serve the marginalized, the poor, the disenfranchised. We respond to the realities of our planet with care, concern and conviction, knowing that if our generation doesn't, our children's earth-home will be one less hospitable and fecund. We leave home only to come back with a greater sense of it, with a greater impression of how to serve it and an inspired way of how to live in it. We live forward with a sense of knowing home.

It is a strange thing to come home. While yet on the journey, you cannot at all realize how strange it will be.
–Selma Lagerlof (1858-1940)

WAYMARKER: HOME AGAIN

Our old world will appear changed and strangified in proportion to how much we changed on our journey. If indeed it was a soulful journey, our former life may be nearly unrecognizable.
–Phil Cousineau

This longing you express is the return message.
-Mevlana Rumi

Loving God, our hearts are restless until they find their rest in you. Help us as we search to combine our gladness with our compassion. Grant us a sense of perspective on our shortcomings, and open our lives to your encompassing joy. We give you thanks for these times of sharing and learning; for your presence in our world and in our lives. Nourish our hearts that we may increasingly make room for love and thereby for your transformative presence. Amen.

Imagine your return journey as the last act of an epic story. Which moments gleamed brighter, gave you pause, challenged all your previous beliefs, reconfirmed your belief in the Power at the center? How did you happen upon them? Were they self-willed, the result of punctilious planning, or were they serendipitous? Did you feel any strange visitations of joy? Can you recapture them now that you are home?

Ask yourself: What difference does it make that you have made this journey? How will others be affected?

_____

_____

_____

WAYMARKER: HOME AGAIN

Now I become myself.
It's taken time,
many years and places....
-May Sarton (1930-1973)

PILGRIMAGE: CENTERING TOOLS

There are various spiritual disciplines that may deepen and enhance your connection with God, others, and yourself while on this pilgrimage. The following resources are provided to you, the pilgrim, with the prayerful hope that they will guide reflection times and also introduce methods of discerning God's will and intent for your life.

Journal Keeping

As we cross the threshold from the mundane into the mentality of the pilgrim, we must begin to listen. We must tune our ear to the essentials of what is being said, and what is not for that matter. A pilgrimage is an opportunity to reconnect with your soul.[30] The discipline of listening well needs to be rehearsed so that the habit is established this side of the departure. Sacred travel is essentially about having the ears to listen for when something tries to reach you–a voice, your calling, your destiny. Begin listening now. Now is also the time to begin your pilgrimage journal. Use the quietest time of your day, whether that be morning before others are stirring, or at night when the city is beginning to sleep. Spend time recalling past journeys and travels; this is a helpful way to discover the motivation behind this particular pilgrimage. Recalling can help clarify the call to come.

PILGRIMAGE: CENTERING TOOLS

Reflection Question(s)

Imagine lighting an old brass lantern. Visualize the light that pours forth over the road in front of you (Psalm 119:105). Think of the ways that questions illuminate the world around us. Questions tune the soul. The purpose behind questions is to initiate the quest. Recall the words of Alan Jones, dean of Grace Cathedral in San Francisco, who writes, "We are impoverished in our longing and devoid of imagination when it comes to our reaching out to others.... We need to be introduced to our longings, because they guard our mystery."[32]

Ask yourself what mystery is being guarded by your longing.

Imagine the last time you truly listened. What are you listening for now? What calls do you hear amid the cacophony of your life? What are you praying for? Recall that inside every question is a quest trying to get out. To get the question, you have to get out.[33]

Imagine your departure as a metamorphosis. Through simple acts of intention and attention, you can transform a [simple act] into a soulful journey. The first step is to slow down. The next one is to treat everything that comes your way as part of the sacred time that envelops your pilgrimage.[34]

_____

_____

_____

_____

PILGRIMAGE: CENTERING TOOLS

As you look back on your life, can you recall times when you have become willing rather than willful toward God, when you have "let go and let God," when you have said, "here am I" in the sense of total willingness? If so, write about how that felt. If not, write what it might mean for you right now – what you think God wants from you right now, what objections and fears you might have, what it is that tugs you to give in to God.

PILGRIMAGE: CENTERING TOOLS

Following is a helpful guide, framed in concise questions, to centering on the God-given value of each day. Honing in on the daily 'value' is a way of discerning God's calling for your life, for in these answers lives evidence of authentic vocational expression.

At the End of the Day: A Mirror of Questions
What dreams did I create last night?
Where did my eyes linger today?
Where was I blind?
Where was I hurt without anyone noticing?
What did I learn today?
What did I read?
What new thoughts visited me?
What differences did I notice in those closest to me?
Whom did I neglect?
Where did I neglect myself?
What did I begin today that might endure?
How were my conversations?
What did I do today for the poor and the excluded?
Did I remember the dead today?
Where could I have exposed myself to the risk of something different?
Where did I allow myself to receive love?
With whom today did I feel the most myself?
What reached me today? How deep did it imprint?
Who saw me today?
What visitations had I from the past and form the future?
What did I avoid today?
From the evidence-why was I given this day?[35]

PILGRIMAGE: CENTERING TOOLS

The discernment process of this pilgrimage will be amplified by the use of journaling. God will be present in the details of the day and it is essential to pay attention! Remember that the day's activities are the starting point for reflection; you may want to write some details of a particular incident as it affected you, but you probably will not list the chronology of your day. After you have thought through the day's events, ask yourself the following questions to start the day's journaling:

- Where today did I specifically see or feel the presence of God working in my life and in the world?
- Was I aware of God at the time? If not, what attitudes or actions were blocking my receptiveness to the Divine?
- In what ways was I able to bring the spirit of Christ to the various parts of my life? How did I fail to show his loving spirit and compassion?
- Were there specific events this day that helped me understand who I am as a follower of Christ?[36]

_____
_____
_____
_____
_____
_____
_____
_____
_____
_____

PILGRIMAGE: CENTERING TOOLS

Another helpful way to begin the journaling process is to complete any of the following thoughts in a free-flowing (stream-of-consciousness) style:

- My life is....
- I am....
- To me, God is...
- I feel God calling me to...
- This pilgrimage represents...
- I saw the Sacred today in...

_____
_____
_____
_____
_____
_____
_____
_____
_____
_____
_____
_____
_____
_____
_____

PILGRIMAGE: CENTERING TOOLS

The Ritual of Lighting Candles

Long ago, every act of making fire was considered sacred, since fire was a gift from the gods. With the invention of electric lighting, the lighting of candles and fires ceased to be a necessity and thus lost much of its awesome power. While we may not think of fire as sacred, we use it at special times in prayer, worship, at meals, and on holidays. With their small tongues of fire, candles speak of warmth, love, celebration. God appeared as fire in many Old Testament stories. The lighting of candles and vigil lights should be more than a means of decoration; it should awaken us to our vocation to be the light of the world. It can be a powerful sign of the presence of God in times of trouble, suffering, storm, and inner darkness as well as times of celebration and great joy.[36]

While at the Iona Abbey, you will have the opportunity to light a candle for your intention, or for the needs of others in your life.

The following rituals for lighting candles provide patterns for personal prayer using light, the most universal and ancient symbol for the mystery we call God.

Lighting a Candle for Prayer or Worship
As I now bring fire to this candle wick,
making it glow with light,
may I also bring the fire of love
to this time of worship.

PILGRIMAGE: CENTERING TOOLS

Candle Prayer at Any Time
Fire is your sacrament, O God, fire is sacred;
as I light this candle may I be reminded
that I am to burn with the same fire for you.
may I fill my life with that burning love.

Candle Prayer at a Time of Darkness (Labyrinth)
O Divine Wisdom, I am confused and unsure;
It feels like I am lost in the darkness.
As I light this candle,
Let your light enter my heart
That I may see the path before me.
May this holy light
Quiet the voices of fear that confuse my judgment
And cloud my heart's true vision.
Grant me the gift of divine wisdom
That I may step forward with faith and courage.

Candle Prayer at a Time of Need for Another
O Gracious God who knows all our needs
And who cares for us daily with such great love,
Be with _____,
Who is in great need of your presence.
I light this candle of prayer
And dedicate it for her (his) needs.
May your light surround her (him);
May your love be her (his) support
And may your life flow through her (him).
I dedicate the actions, prayers, and duties of my day
For her (his) needs at this special time. [37]

PILGRIMAGE: CENTERING TOOLS

The Examen

Search me, O God, and know my heart;
test me and know my thoughts.
See if there is any wicked way in me,
and lead me in the way everlasting.
Psalm 139:23-24

The Examen comes to us from the Jesuit spiritual tradition; St. Ignatius wrote The Spiritual Exercises, which has guided this tradition and retreatants for centuries. St. Ignatius believed that the method of The Examen was a gift from God that was meant to enrich his Christian life; it was a way to seek and find God in all things and to gain the freedom to let God's will be done on earth. This way of praying allowed Ignatius to discover the voice of God within his own heart and to experience the ability to discern and become familiar with God's will. He expected that God would speak through our deepest feelings and yearnings, what he called "consolation" and "desolation." Consolation is whatever helps us connect with ourselves, others, God and the universe. Desolation is whatever disconnects us. By returning to our deepest moments of consolation and desolation, we are able to assess patterns and behaviors (positive and negative) that hinder and/or move the Spirit in our life. This can be a very helpful method to discerning God's will and intention.

Behind this practice of self-examination lies a very basic assumption: we have made a choice to offer ourselves to God's service, and we have an active desire to live in God's presence, being led by the Spirit each day. We examine our

PILGRIMAGE: CENTERING TOOLS

minds and hearts in order to see clearly where we have been led, when we have had a sense of God's presence, and where or when we have lost that connection. Questions can guide us: How has God been present to me through the people and situations I have encountered this day? Have I been aware of divine presence? Where have I been responding to the Spirit today? Where have I not responded? Why? [38]

There are many ways that one can begin the process of self-examination; it is common to use a prayer time, journaling, or even time with others to contextualize the practice. Ben Campbell Johnson speaks of learning to "pray with our lives." He suggests a basic process to integrate the prayer life with the ordinary events of our days:

-Gather the day. Identify significant events of your day, including prayer, conversation, meetings, meals, work, etc. List them.

-Review the day. Reflect upon the occurrences listed, without judging yourself, avoiding feelings, or making excuses. This is the actual substance of your daily life.

-Give thanks for the day. Thank God for each part of your day, for your life, and for God's presence in the midst of it.

-Confess your sin. Acknowledge your faults in thought, word, and deed toward God, your neighbor, creation, and yourself.

-Seek the meaning of the events. Reflect on the larger significance of each event. What is God saying to me?

PILGRIMAGE: CENTERING TOOLS

What am I being called to do? How is this connected to the rest of my life?[39]

Following are a list of alternative questions that can be used to articulate your daily consolation(s) and desolation(s)[40]:

For what moment today am I most grateful?
For what moment today am I least grateful?

There are many ways to ask the same questions:

When did I give and receive the most love today?
When did I give and receive the least love today?

When did I feel most alive today?
When did I most feel life draining out of me?

When today did I have the greatest sense of belonging to myself, others, God and the universe?
When did I have the least sense of belonging?

When was I happiest today?
When was I saddest?

What was today's high point?
What was today's low point?

PILGRIMAGE: CENTERING TOOLS

Holy Listening

The art of making travel sacred is very much about listening for God in all stages of the trip. We tune our inner ear for the Spirit's voice, intentionally listening for direction, promptings, or holy invitations. During the pilgrimage stage of transformation (or labyrinth), there is always an element of inner conflict or struggle. It is time spent in the wilderness within, where you meet your fears and confront them-where you come up against whatever prevents you from hearing the voice of the Spirit, or living a life of compassion and generosity. The pilgrim knows that there is no growth without inner confrontation, no promised land without time in the wilderness, no mountaintop that can be reached without goring through the valley of the shadow of death.[41]

In sacred travel, every experience is imbued with the Holy; no encounter is without meaning. There are signs everywhere, if only we learn how to read them. God will speak to us through many a messenger-when we meet a stranger, or even a strange behavior-on the road. But we must be listening![42]

I weave a silence onto my lips,
I weave a silence into my mind,
I weave a silence within my heart.
I close my ears to distractions,
I close my eyes to attractions.
I close my heart to temptations.
-Celtic saying

PILGRIMAGE: CENTERING TOOLS

Silence

Settle yourself in solitude and you will come upon [God] in yourself.
–Teresa of Avila

Our normal lives are filled with amplified sound coming at us from all perspectives. There are the very real noises of planes, trains and automobiles. Then there are the myriad of subtle sounds-cell phones, text messages, Instant Messaging, and other modes of media. The demands of relationships can also offer up their own version of needy noise-your parents need you to call them, your roommate needs your time, a child cries for your care. We pilgrimage to leave behind the normal structures of life to engage the Holy; we also must leave behind the noise so to better hear God.

The rhythm of Iona will lend itself to times of solitude and silence; even community times will convey a sense of discernment and listening. Simply to refrain from talking, without a heart listening to God, is not silence. "A day filled with noise and voices can be a day of silence, if the noises become for us the echo of the presence of God. When we speak of ourselves and are filled with ourselves, we leave silence behind. When we repeat the intimate words of God that he has left within us, our silence remains intact."[43]

PILGRIMAGE: CENTERING TOOLS

Cultivate quiet-space while on Iona. Since you are likely to only be walking while on the island, intentionally set out for solitude walks. Hike the heathered hills in silence. Set the lines of quietude about yourself, not to exclude others, but to maintain the listening ear. The intention here is to make it the practice to be in silence, so that silence is easier found than conversation. Like Jesus, we must go away from people and find places of solitude and silence. This space allows for us to "listen to God's speech in his wondrous, terrible, gentle, loving, all-embracing silence."[44]

PILGRIMAGE: CENTERING TOOLS

Lectio Divina

For any pilgrim, sacred texts are an essential component for the preparation of arrival. We must read these elemental truths in a specialized and practiced way so that the inspired text becomes animate and meaningful. Reading in the quest for God-or reading for holiness-has traditionally been called *lectio divina*. Literally, it means "divine reading" or "sacred reading." The primary source of what is read in lectio divina is Sacred Scripture. Secondarily, lectio refers to the reading of other texts recognized as holy by the Christian community.[45]

Lectio as a form of vocalization lends itself naturally to repetition of particular words and phrases, and such a repetition does in fact become part of the very technique of reading for holiness. Thus the consoling word, the arresting phrase, the sentence that challenges us to the core, is repeated over and over again, and, if consigned to memory, remains forever available. The purpose of lectio is not memorization however; repetition is the process by which the Word of God permeates and nourishes us. A metaphor to describe lectio is that of eating. You take a bite of food, you chew the morsel, you taste and savor it, and ultimately it is swallowed-nourishing the body. As one repeats the sacred text (out loud), the phrase is chewed-repeated over and over- and ruminated on, pondered. Through the reading, through the repetition, we ultimately are led into a discourse with the Divine. Done properly, lectio divina is a form of reading that leads to prayer.[46]

PILGRIMAGE: CENTERING TOOLS

The pilgrim's journey is as much an interior one as the roads on which she walks. We traverse the globe to reach our sacred site, but it is the inner landscape of our soul that must be navigated to arrive at our ultimate goal: connection with God. Lectio Divina is a rewarding tradition to practice with the intention of making space for conversation with the Creator.

PILGRIMAGE: CENTERING TOOLS

Centering Prayer

Another contemplative prayer practice is Centering Prayer. This method for prayer does not rely on the use of images or any sort of visual aid (i.e. icons, pictures, books). Thomas Keating describes Centering Prayer in this way:

Centering prayer is a method designed to deepen the relationship with Christ begun, for example, in lectio divina and to facilitate the development of contemplative prayer by preparing our faculties to cooperate with this gift. It is an attempt to present the teaching of earlier times (e.g. the Cloud of Unknowing) in an updated form and to put a certain order and regularity into it. It is not meant to replace other kinds of prayer; it simply puts other kinds of prayer into a new and fuller perspective. During the time of prayer, we consent to Cod's presence and action within. At other times our attention moves outward to discover God's presence everywhere else.[47]

PILGRIMAGE: CENTERING TOOLS

The Guidelines for Centering Prayer:

1. Choose a sacred word as the symbol of your intention to consent to God's presence and action within.

2. Sitting comfortably and with eyes closed, settle briefly, and silently introduce the sacred word as the symbol of your consent to God's presence and action within.

3. When you become aware of thoughts, return ever so gently to the sacred word.

4. At the end of the prayer period, remain in silence with eyes closed for a couple of minutes.

Centering Prayer is normally practiced for 20 minutes twice a day, usually after rising in the morning and again before the evening meal at the end of the day.[48]

REFLECTIONS

REFLECTIONS

REFLECTIONS

REFLECTIONS

REFLECTIONS

REFLECTIONS

REFLECTIONS

SOURCES AND ACKNOWLEDGEMENTS

1. E. Mairi MacArthur, Iona-The Living Memory of a Crofting Community, (Edinburgh, Scotland: Polygon: 1990, 2002), ix.

2. This paragraph is a paraphrase of P. Sheldrake's reflections on Celtic themes and Iona being a prime example of these examples in one place. Philip Sheldrake, Living Between Worlds-Place and Journey in Celtic Spirituality (Boston, MA: Cowley Publications: 1996), 84.

3. Phil Cousineau, The Art of Pilgrimage, (Boston, MA: Conari Press, 1998), xxiii.

4. Ibid., xxiv.

5. These compiled stages of pilgrimage-and their descriptions-have been taken from Phil Cousineau's The Art of Pilgrimage and Sarah York's Pilgrim Heart, The Inner Journey Home, (San Francisco: Jossey-Bass, 2001).

6. Sarah York, Pilgrim Heart: The Inner Journey Home, (San Francisco: Jossey-Bass, 2001), 5.

7. Elizabeth Canham, Praying the Bible, (Forward Movement Publications: 1987, 2001) 95, 96.

8. Phil Cousineau, The Art of Pilgrimage, (Boston, MA: Conari Press, 1998), 63.

9. Sarah York, Pilgrim Heart: The Inner Journey Home, (San

SOURCES
AND ACKNOWLEDGEMENTS

Francisco: Jossey-Bass, 2001), 6.

10. Ibid.,10

11. John O'Donohue, To Bless the Space Between Us, (Doubleday; 2008).

12. Sarah York, Pilgrim Heart: The Inner Journey Home, (San Francisco: Jossey-Bass, 2001),13.

13. Phil Cousineau, The Art of Pilgrimage, (Boston, MA: Conari Press, 1998), 96.

14. Ibid., 83.

15. Ibid., 98.

16. Elizabeth Canham, Praying the Bible, (Forward Movement Publications; 1987, 2001), 103.

17. Sarah York, Pilgrim Heart: The Inner Journey Home, (San Francisco: Jossey-Bass, 2001),12.

18. Phil Cousineau, The Art of Pilgrimage, (Boston, MA: Conari Press, 1998), 134.

19. Ibid.,132.

20. Ibid., 197.

SOURCES AND ACKNOWLEDGEMENTS

21. Robert Pinsky, *Canto 1,* from *The Inferno of Dante: A New Verse Translation* (New York: Noonday Press, 1994), canto 1: 1-7.

22. Phil Cousineau, The Art of Pilgrimage, (Boston, MA: Conari Press, 1998), 163.

23. Ibid., 216

24. Phil Cousineau, The Art of Pilgrimage, (Boston, MA: Conari Press, 1998), 217.

24. Sarah York, Pilgrim Heart: The Inner Journey Home, (San Francisco: Jossey-Bass, 2001),149.

25. Phil Cousineau, The Art of Pilgrimage, (Boston, MA: Conari Press, 1998), 87.

26. Earth Ministry, Caring For All Creation: By the Waters, Ed. LeeAnne Beres, 2007.

27. Eriugena, Periphyseon 554B

28. "Wanderlust Travel Awards announced". Wanderlust. 2009-02-05. Retrieved on 2009-07-29

29. The castle was used as a location in the 1999 movie Entrapment starring Sean Connery and Catherine Zeta-Jones

SOURCES AND ACKNOWLEDGEMENTS

30. Phil Cousineau, The Art of Pilgrimage, (Boston, MA: Conari Press, 1998), 24.

31. Phil Cousineau, The Art of Pilgrimage, (Boston, MA: Conari Press, 1998), 88.

32. Phil Cousineau, The Art of Pilgrimage, (Boston, MA: Conari Press, 1998), 71.

33. Thirsty for God: A Brief History of Christian Spirituality, 2nd Edition; Bradley P. Holt; Fortress Press, 2005, 177-178.

34. Anne Broyles, Journaling-A Spirit Journey, (Nashville, TN: The Upper Room, 1988), 13-14.

35. Anne Broyles, Journaling-A Spirit Journey, (Nashville, TN: The Upper Room, 1988), 24.

36. Edward Hays, Prayers for a Planetary Pilgrim, (Notre Dame, IN: Forest of Peace, 1998, 2008), 267.

37. All candle prayers are from Edward Hays', Prayers for a Planetary Pilgrim, (Notre Dame, IN: Forest of Peace, 1998, 2008), 267-269.

38. Marjorie J. Thompson, Soul Feast-An Invitation to the Christian Spiritual Life, (Louisville, KY: Westminster John Knox Press, 1995, 2005), 100-101.

SOURCES AND ACKNOWLEDGEMENTS

39. These quotes and the following paraphrase of process are taken from Ben Campbell Johnson's, Invitation to Pray (Decatur, GA: CTS Press, 1992), 18-22.

40. Dennis Linn, Sheila Fabricant Linn, Matthew Linn, Sleeping with Bread-Holding What Gives You Life, (Mahwah, NJ: Paulist Press, 1995), 6-7.

41. Sarah York, Pilgrim Heart: The Inner Journey Home, (San Francisco: Jossey-Bass, 2001), 12.

42. A paraphrase of statements made by Phil Cousineau, The Art of Pilgrimage, (Boston, MA: Conari Press, 1998), 97.

43. Richard J. Foster, Celebration of Discipline (San Francisco, CA: 1978, 1988, 1998), 98.

44. A quote from Doherty in Richard J. Foster's, Celebration of Discipline (San Francisco, CA: 1978, 1988, 1998), 109.

45. Robin Maas and Gabriel O'Donnell, Spiritual Traditions for the Contemporary Church (Nashville, TN: Abingder Press, 1990), 45.

46. Paraphrase of sections from Robin Maas and Gabriel O'Donnel's, Spiritual Traditions for the Contemporary Church (Nashville, TN: Abingder Press, 1990), 46-47.

SOURCES AND ACKNOWLEDGEMENTS

47. Thomas Keating, Open Mind, Open Heart, (Continuum International Publishing Group: 1986) 39.

48. Kyrie.com, http://www.kyrie.com/cp/, Guidelines for Centering Prayer; May 10, 2008.

Made in the USA
Middletown, DE
10 October 2017